REFUGIA

To Patrick —
With ever-so much gratitude
for noticing the fine lines in
the world, and lending some
to this little book.

Love,

[signature]

March 2019
Portland, OR

REFUGIA

KRISTIN BERGER

Persian Pony Press/Portland, Oregon

Cover illustration "Untitled Abstract 2018" by Patrick Barber
@blackletterheart.

The definition of refugium comes from *Home Ground: Language for an American Landscape,* edited by Barry Lopez and Debra Gwartney, Trinity University Press, 2006.

"Indian Caves in the Dry Country," William Stafford, *Someday, Maybe,* Harper & Row Publishers, Inc., 1973.

Gratitude to the editors of *The Inflectionist Review,* John Sibley Williams and Anatoly Molotkov, who gave sections of this work a home within their journal, and for their generous editorial feedback. To Playa at Summer Lake, for the gift of space and time and beauty to work on poems during the Spring of 2017, and to Oma and Lindy, for their cabin along the banks of the White Salmon River, where the manuscript was completed in the Winter of 2018. To Katharine Salzmann, for her design and editorial guidance, for everything. And to Scot Siegel, who helped these poems along through ice & snow, darkness & light.

Sections of *Refugia* were nominated by *The Inflectionist Review* for The Pushcart Prize and The Best of the Net, 2017.

for S

refugium; *n, pl* -gia:

A biological refuge. The realm of the unintended, the hidden, the inadvertent pocket of protection where species large and small often find their lives least disturbed.

These are some canyons
we might use again
sometime.

William Stafford

1/ SNOW ON EARTH

1

When winter runs out,
who will hold the night clock?
Will the heart know to slow,
stop roaming and skipping beats?
The earth prefers part-time awakeness,
tilts to jut our time capsules off its hot hide.
At sea level, snow comes
to smother us into dreaming.

in the warm November garden
we have been young
too long

2

Stunned at our windows,
the sky tantrums, pitching sleet.
Junkyard wire razors a white music
beyond the auto crusher,
the city's collapse; wind
blindsides ditch willows, tries
to knock the smallest bird
from her heartbeat.

we sleep apart for seasons
hands tracing the bucking melt
of sweet dark loam

3

Trenches connected us then, four foot deep
cross-cuts of the week's blizzard.
Our fathers dug us out. Wet and red-cheeked,
we stomped at each other's doors—
Always evening in the whipped blue drifts.
Dead grass, dug down, became our muffled fires.
Icicles we snapped from gutters
and licked into marshmallow spears.
It didn't have to end. Our mother's voices
shouldn't have been able to reach us,
but they did; called us out, called us in.

meet me in the snow meadow
with the frozen pond skirting the woodlot
the one between childhoods

4

Hummingbirds bench at iced feeders
by the torpor of taillights.
Snow blots the air like triggered pigeons.
Wind uproots trees mostly for the fox.
Beneath shelves of slate, far off in the mountains
moths whir the alarm of heat's buckshot—
bears claw out, feed and fatten like apples.
We thaw one day, then the next, skyshot.

between lip and tongue
secret spring's
oxalis leaf

5

Living so long under a blue sky veined
by contrails, we begin to believe in retreat.
The silent phone. Highway cleared of rumble.
Diesel-loaded dreams plowed in the dead of winter
and parking lot gulls swarm the grit-heaped banks.
The atmospheric river has plans for us.
Morning storms and the marriage bed
is stripped, snow-blind.

dream of walleye under black ice
a notation of air bubbles
sealed dark and its promise

6

On the north side of July's slope
under a huckleberry wind
patches of snow survive.
Refugia. Glacier lilies divide
deep beneath the blankets.
We couple like a storm buckling,
seeds of dust, cloud to core.
We fall. Supersaturated lore.
You drift in. I avalanche.
Banks bury the ways
we have known each other.

apple blossoms
have yet to fall away
time is our coalbed

Tell me about water.
Do you call it *creek* or *crik,*
stream or *brook?*
Pull the blinds up
when it pours
or turn from what comes?
Take the clothes off the line
or let ozone soak?
Will you recite our stories
about that night we tailgated rain,
frogs crossing the road so thickly
you had to slow to a swerve
while vernal pools filled with slide
and mount and lust and trill
and we filled, too, with calm,
like the thinnest rivulet
hydroplaning?

browse like deer
on green shoots
help my thaw along

8

Where there's flocking, there's water,
white cloud of fuss and arrangement.
Where there's a dirt road, there's us,
windows rolled down, listening.
An open weir's rush. A faint lapping.
Water gathered around the ankles of herons.
The reservoir appears, its alkali and shell-baked
rings holding a memory of blue
flooding the reeds—the future so full
and near, so swimmable and sweet.

snowmelt scours
the persistent boulder
river's assurance

Dawn tats a banded blue
to our breathing, our waking.
I pull you into me
like the swallow that rescues
blue yarn from the wrackline
for her nest of moss
a low-hanging cotton ornament
at the river wayside. Like her,
we might save the world, or,
at least, the rough light.

the animal in me
hunts for a time before
it all began

We make love by turning towards.
All the body cannot turn away from.
Our ever-climb and squint. Sun's salutation.
Willow leaf on its axis. Breath to word.
Palm to hip. Lip to jaw. The many-night expressions
of wind sliding over a roof. The river rushes
toward its future with slant and resolve;
so much love enters from hidden runnels,
we cannot help but widen.

the meadow is my desert
I roll the moon in my mouth
when I want water

11

We are near-threatened.
The Au Sauble should be iced-over,
hemmed by young jack pine and birch.
We could walk all day missing
the Kirtland warbler, soft bevel of gold
clinging to summer's tough bark.
Let's self-resuscitate, keep our chins up.
There still may be time. Over the Bahamas,
they are long gone, flying figure eights,
trading our New World apologies
for their old, blue-washed paradise.

lace up and stand with me
no river breakup
inch out and lock hands

12

Spring's dartboard strike.
Birch girdled by hunger.
Snow gives way to a longing
to be held, not just once,
but enveloped, a valley of nights.
You never come to my bed anymore.
The thought of someone else's hip
crumbles me like dirt flush with hellebore.
The river, throttled.
Soon, ice will heave the silence,
take out bridges, free the perfect houses,
leave our escarpment so clean.

love is protest
it can hold
what clouds threat down

2/ EARTH ON FIRE

13

Before, when we were all under water,
fire didn't know how to call out to itself—
no strike-everywhere thirsty cornice
no gravel-bar moss bed linger
no deadwood to kindle
against the blue tarp of sky;
ice dam rushing from the Divide; sun,
a pebble perfecting its tumble.

plume of blue smoke
in the foothills, nearly as kind
as a kestrel's stall

14

How, under a turf of wind and sun-scour,
do the Badlands not wear themselves out?
Where is the nub of the old mountain's backbone
still consenting to carry us, year after year?
My first taste of sage was at the bottom of a draw
where water seeped black through ancestral chalk,
and when I tilted my chin
a cascading thicket of meadowlarks
fanned the only green for miles.

on the shale-slick ridge
do not leave the trail
for anything

15

Fire begins with *Yes,* hungry
like a newborn, blazing every
notch, limb and canyon
pivoting towards the source.
We nurture a coalbed from space,
shunt the small sparks
of ash-clogged creeks,
protests of *Now*
runneling to the refuge of sea
rising to meet.

wrackline of hot springs
and dusk holds us
to the tilt

16

The pastille of sun
smoldering under tongue,
acrid brick, placebo of shine—
breathe into wet bandanas,
long for a rain-tamped bed
of exhales, skin to skin
collaborating an exit
until the smoke clears.

ash billows from the curb
thick on next year's
raspberry bed

Like sleepwalkers, like us,
like teasel combing wind—
a nearly silent midnight
beneath the roar.
Between curtains of fire,
killdeer thread the river—
a back channel, gravel bar,
taupes and pebble grays.
Rain is months away.
Do they catch the scent
of earth thirsting
to be pooled?

breaststroke and trust
the last glacier
melting beneath us

18

When smoke-blind in a firestorm,
rely on dim sun-whorl and the thunder
of horses climbing over their stalls
towards a slot of calm,
any day that comes
out of the blue.

nightjars trust
desert constellations
with the whole of their lives

At 2000 feet, snow overwhelms
the last hot-spot, 100% contained.
Returned to heartwood-sleep, firs receive
each flake like ash homing
where the drama began.
They pitch spears into the white
skeletal reef cooled by billows
of freezing fog, the clamor
of summer extinguished.

a cloud drifts up-river
barge of carefully
worded dreams

Cold weans water from Devonian gravel
and pipes without lamp bulbs
nestled underneath freeze by morning.
Forget fire, forget the Gypsy Moth
and the infestation of heat,
groves of white pines giving up
sap and song. Remember
the long black drink of well-water,
the slide into the lake, the mineral way
earth wants us back.

after ice
what will our tongues
cling to

Never has the highway sounded so thin,
like the night-sigh of a braid unraveling
or static between stations, between storms.
Air has lost its oceanic swell.
Remember how every sense brimmed
lying next to each other; perched
above the basin, how the air was a lake
and we could breathe underwater?
How time stretched our heat like a tarmac.

lakes on fire
wait for snow
to fall home

22

Always the last night on earth.
The kiss found us like a star of snow
not wanting to land.
Curbs lay all around.
Traffic did not notice us.
Wind avalanched with no endpoint,
gathering steam in the wake of city buses.
Let's be found, imperfectly
leaning into our first intersection.

walk the lakebed's
puzzle-cracks
miles without me

Pools appear where water hasn't reached in years.
Cliffs release and plait all they cannot hold,
white upon basalt against moss's chartreuse stain.
It takes only the sky remembering to let go.
We may never be touched again
quite like this spring loves the earth.
Pull off at the road's wide shoulder,
where the river swells to unmoor willows
and unnerve train tracks—
Wind blusters its storage of grit
and the busy chips of warblers.
Everything is drawn to a body.

you didn't know
we could flow so strong
through the map of replenishment

24

In 100 years, we'll have left the trail.
No living story. How we loved.
How the world still shifts from our steps.
Each route, a charred blueprint unscrolling us.
Snow on the ridge, never an end in sight.
Water slows to the speed of memory,
fills kettle lakes with blue proof.
Children will skip through willow sundials
and the legends of bears' large hearts
just to climb this terminal moraine,
feel the sun burning.

edge-tree at the blowdown
leaning like a fort
our kind, so rare

Kristin Berger is the author of the poetry collections *Echolocation* (Cirque Press, 2018), *How Light Reaches Us* (Aldrich Press, 2016), and a poetry chapbook, *For the Willing* (Finishing Line Press, 2008). Her long prose-poem *Changing Woman & Changing Man: A High Desert Myth,* was a finalist for the 2016 Newfound Prose Prize. She lives in Portland, Oregon.

Persian Pony Press is a pop-up press based in Portland, Oregon. The Persian pony comes from a figure in Federico García Lorca's poem *Gacela del Amor Imprevisto.*

Made in the USA
Middletown, DE
07 March 2019